D1324503

SUPER SIMPLE
HOLIDAY
cookies

EASY COOKIE RECIPES FOR KIDS!

ALEX KUSKOWSKI

Consulting Editor, Diane Craig, M.A./Reading Specialist

Super Sandcastle

An Imprint of Abdo Publishing
abdopublishing.com

abdopublishing.com

Published by Abdo Publishing, a division of ABDO, PO Box 398166, Minneapolis, Minnesota 55439. Copyright © 2016 by Abdo Consulting Group, Inc. International copyrights reserved in all countries. No part of this book may be reproduced in any form without written permission from the publisher. Super SandCastle™ is a trademark and logo of Abdo Publishing.

Printed in the United States of America, North Mankato, Minnesota
102015
012016

Editor: Liz Salzmann
Content Developer: Nancy Tuminelly
Cover and Interior Design and Production: Mighty Media, Inc.
Photo Credits: Mighty Media, Inc. and Shutterstock

The following manufacturers/names appearing in this book are trademarks: Arm & Hammer®, Brer Rabbit®, C&H®, Crisco®, Hershey®, Market Pantry™, McCormick®, Pillsbury®, Proctor Silex ®

Library of Congress Cataloging-in-Publication Data
Kuskowski, Alex, author.
  Super simple holiday cookies : easy cookie recipes for kids! / Alex Kuskowski.
    pages cm. -- (Super simple cookies)
  ISBN 978-1-62403-949-2
1. Cookies--Juvenile literature. 2. Holiday cooking--Juvenile literature. 3. Baking--Juvenile literature. I. Title.
  TX772.K777 2016
  641.86'54--dc23
            2015020594

Super SandCastle™ books are created by a team of professional educators, reading specialists, and content developers around five essential components—phonemic awareness, phonics, vocabulary, text comprehension, and fluency—to assist young readers as they develop reading skills and strategies and increase their general knowledge. All books are written, reviewed, and leveled for guided reading and early reading intervention programs for use in shared, guided, and independent reading and writing activities to support a balanced approach to literacy instruction.

TO ADULT HELPERS

Help your child learn to cook! Cooking lets children practice math and science. It teaches kids about responsibility and boosts their confidence. Plus they get to make some great food!

Before getting started, set ground rules for using the kitchen, cooking tools, and ingredients. There should always be adult supervision when use of a sharp tool, oven, or stove is required. Be aware of the symbols below that indicate when special care is necessary.

So, put on your apron and get ready to cheer on your new chef!

. . . .

SYMBOLS
. . . .

Hot!
This recipe requires the use of a stove or oven. You will need adult supervision and assistance.

Sharp!
This recipe includes the use of a sharp utensil such as a knife or grater. Ask an adult to help out.

. . . .

CONTENTS

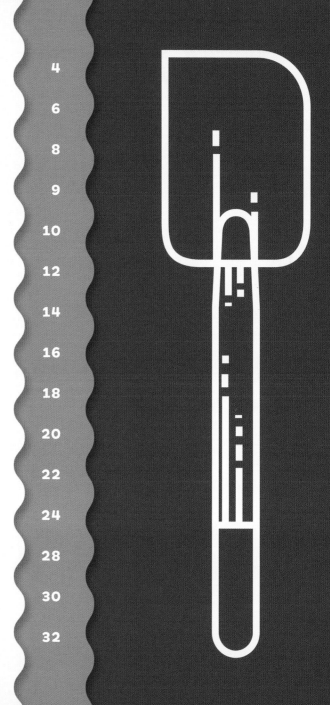

Holiday Fun Cookies	4
Cooking Basics	6
Measuring Ingredients	8
Did You Know This = That?	9
Cooking Terms	10
Kitchen Utensils	12
Ingredients	14
New Year's Surprise!	16
Be Mine Hearts	18
Earth Day Globes	20
4th of July Fireworks	22
Spooky Eye Candy	24
Sugary Dreidel Pops	28
Candy Cane Twists	30
Glossary	32

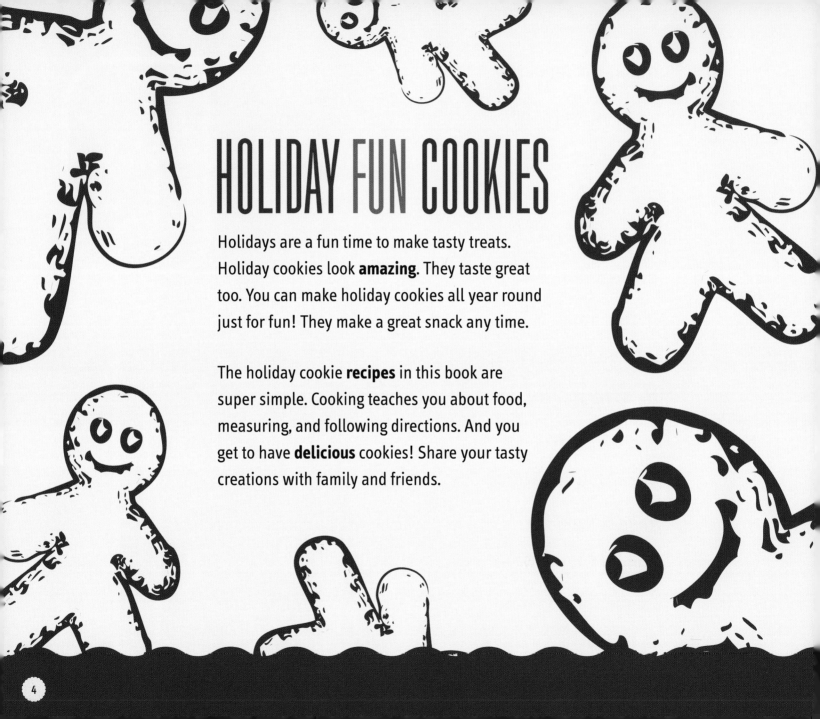

HOLIDAY FUN COOKIES

Holidays are a fun time to make tasty treats. Holiday cookies look **amazing**. They taste great too. You can make holiday cookies all year round just for fun! They make a great snack any time.

The holiday cookie **recipes** in this book are super simple. Cooking teaches you about food, measuring, and following directions. And you get to have **delicious** cookies! Share your tasty creations with family and friends.

 # COOKING BASICS

Think Safety!

- Ask an adult to help you use a knife. Place things on a cutting board to cut them.

- Clean up spills right away.

- Keep things away from the edge of the table or **counter**.

- Ask an adult to help you use the oven.

- Ask for help if you cannot reach something.

Using the Oven

- Preheat the oven while making the **recipe**.

- Use oven-safe dishes.

- Use pot holders or oven mitts to hold hot things.

- Do not touch the oven door. It can be very hot.

- Set a timer. Check the food and bake longer if needed.

Before Baking

- Get **permission** from an adult.

- Wash your hands.

- Read the recipe at least once.

- Set out the ingredients and tools you will need.

- Keep a **towel** close by for cleaning up spills.

When You're Done

- Let the cookies cool completely.

- Store the cookies in **containers**. Put a sheet of waxed paper in between the **layers** of cookies.

- Put all the ingredients and tools away.

- Wash all the dishes and **utensils**. Clean up your work space.

MEASURING INGREDIENTS

Wet Ingredients

Set a measuring cup on the **counter**. Add the liquid. Stop when it reaches the amount you need. Check the measurement from eye level.

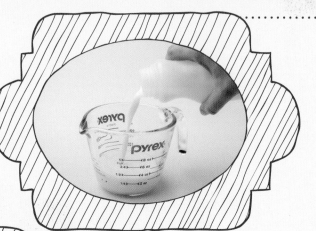

Dry Ingredients

Dip the measuring cup or spoon into the dry ingredient. Fill it with a little more than you need. Use the back of a dinner knife to remove the extra.

Moist Ingredients

Measure ingredients such as brown sugar and dried fruit differently. Press them down into the measuring cup.

DID YOU KNOW THIS = THAT?

There are different ways to measure the same amount.

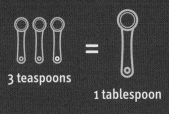

3 teaspoons = 1 tablespoon

4 tablespoons = ¼ cup

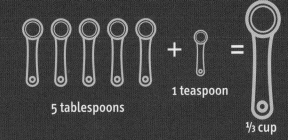

5 tablespoons + 1 teaspoon = ⅓ cup

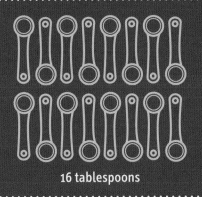

16 tablespoons = 1 cup

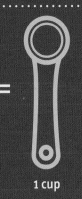

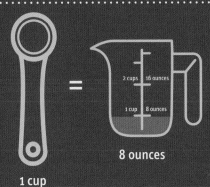

1 cup = 8 ounces

1 stick of butter = ½ cup

2 cups = 1 pint

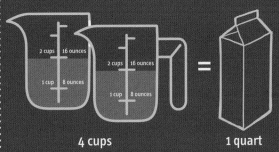

4 cups = 1 quart

2 quarts = ½ gallon

9

COOKING TERMS

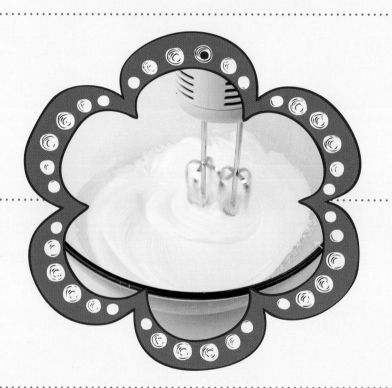

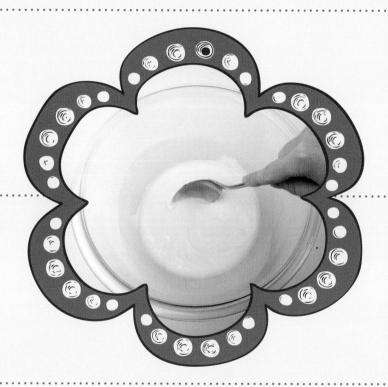

CREAM

Cream means to beat butter and sugar together until light and **fluffy**.

MELT

Melt means to heat something until it is soft or liquid.

STIR

Stir means to mix ingredients together,
usually with a spoon or rubber spatula.

SPREAD

Spread means to make a smooth **layer**
with a spoon, knife, or rubber spatula.

KITCHEN UTENSILS

lollipop sticks

toothpicks

measuring spoons

measuring cups

small bowl

baking sheet

pot holders

microwave-safe bowl

plastic bottle caps

sharp knife

spatula

mixing spoon

waxed paper

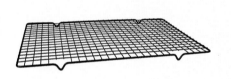

parchment paper

cooling rack

mixing bowls

electric mixer

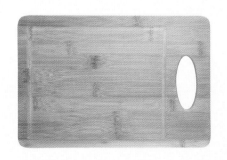

cutting board

INGREDIENTS

all-purpose flour

baking soda

blue sprinkles

brown sugar

butter

canola oil

cocoa powder

colored sprinkles

eggs

food coloring

gold sprinkles

ground cinnamon

ground cloves

ground ginger

heart sprinkles

Hershey's Kisses

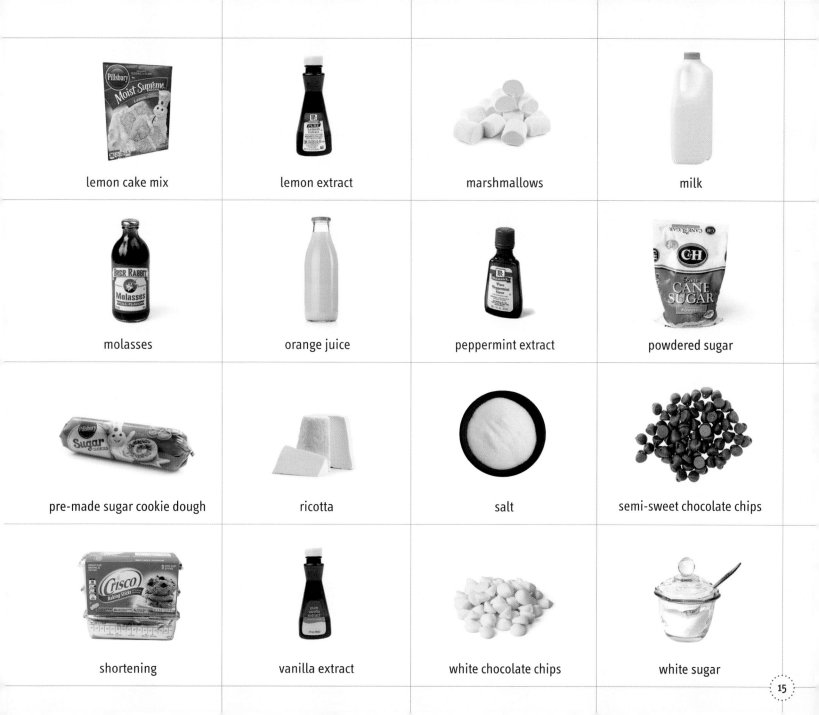lemon cake mix	lemon extract	marshmallows	milk
molasses	orange juice	peppermint extract	powdered sugar
pre-made sugar cookie dough	ricotta	salt	semi-sweet chocolate chips
shortening	vanilla extract	white chocolate chips	white sugar

new
year's
surprise!

MAKES 4 SANDWICHES

INGREDIENTS

pre-made sugar cookie
  dough
1 cup powdered sugar
colored sprinkles
gold sprinkles

. . . .

TOOLS

baking sheets
parchment paper
sharp knife
cutting board
plastic bottle cap
pot holders
spatula
cooling rack
measuring cup
mixing bowl
mixing spoon
dinner knife

1 Preheat the oven to 350 degrees. Cover the baking sheets with parchment paper.

2 Cut the sugar cookie dough into 12 ½-inch (1.3 cm) **slices**. Use a bottle cap to cut a hole in the center of three cookies. Place the cookies on the baking sheet. Bake according to the directions on the package. Put the cookies on a cooling rack.

3 Put the powdered sugar and 1 tablespoon water in a small bowl. Stir.

4 Spread frosting on a cookie that doesn't have a hole. Put a cookie with a hole on top of the frosted cookie. Fill the hole with sprinkles.

5 Frost both sides of another cookie without a hole. Put the second frosted cookie on top of the cookie with a hole.

6 Sprinkle gold sprinkles on top of the cookie.

7 Repeat steps 4 through 6 to make three more sandwich cookies.

MAKES 36 COOKIES

INGREDIENTS

1 cup butter
1 cup white sugar
1 cup brown sugar
2 eggs
2 teaspoons vanilla extract
2 tablespoons milk
2 cups all-purpose flour
½ cup cocoa powder
1 teaspoon baking soda
2 cups heart sprinkles

. . . .

TOOLS

baking sheets
parchment paper
measuring cups
measuring spoons
mixing bowls
electric mixer
spatula
cooling rack

1   Preheat the oven to 350 degrees. Cover the baking sheets with parchment paper.

2   Cream the butter and both sugars in a mixing bowl. Mix in the eggs, vanilla, and milk.

3   Mix the flour, cocoa, and baking soda in a second mixing bowl. Then mix the flour mixture into the sugar mixture.

4   Put the heart sprinkles in a small bowl. Roll the dough into 1-inch (2.5 cm) balls. Coat each ball with sprinkles. Place the balls on the baking sheets.

5   Bake for 10 minutes. Put the cookies on a cooling rack.

earth day globes

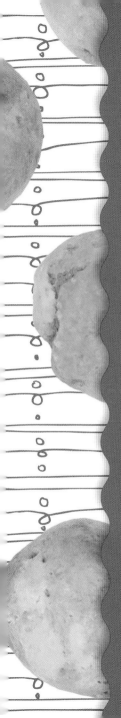

INGREDIENTS

¼ cup butter
1 cup ricotta
1 large egg
1 teaspoon lemon extract
1 package lemon cake mix
blue and green food
   coloring

. . . .

TOOLS

baking sheets
parchment paper
measuring cups
measuring spoons
mixing bowls
electric mixer
pot holders
spatula
cooling rack

1   Preheat the oven to 350 degrees. Cover the baking sheets with parchment paper.

2   Put the butter and ricotta in a medium bowl. Beat with an electric mixer. Mix in the egg and lemon extract.

3   Add the cake mix. Mix well.

4   Put half of the dough in a separate bowl. Add blue food coloring to one bowl. Add green food coloring to the other bowl. Mix the food coloring into the dough. Refrigerate both bowls of dough for 15 minutes.

5   Roll the dough into 1-inch (2.5 cm) balls. Use some of each color in each ball. Put the balls on the baking sheets.

6   Bake for 12 minutes. Put the cookies on a cooling rack.

4th of july
fireworks

INGREDIENTS

2¼ cups all-purpose flour

2 teaspoons ground ginger

1 teaspoon baking soda

¾ teaspoon ground cinnamon

½ teaspoon ground cloves

½ teaspoon salt

¾ cup butter

1 cup white sugar

1 egg

1 tablespoon orange juice

¼ cup molasses

1 cup powdered sugar

food coloring

. . . .

TOOLS

baking sheets

parchment paper

measuring cups

measuring spoons

mixing bowls

mixing spoon

electric mixer

pot holders

spatula

cooling rack

toothpicks

1. Preheat the oven to 350 degrees. Cover the baking sheets with parchment paper.

2. Put the flour, ginger, baking soda, cinnamon, cloves, and salt in a large bowl. Stir.

3. Mix the butter and sugar together in a medium bowl. Mix in the egg, orange juice, and molasses. Slowly mix the molasses mixture into the flour mixture. Refrigerate the dough for 30 minutes.

4. Roll the dough into 1-inch (2.5 cm) balls. Put the balls on the baking sheets. Press them flat. Bake for 10 minutes. Put the cookies on a cooling rack.

5. Put the powdered sugar and 1 tablespoon water in a bowl to make frosting. Mix. **Divide** the mixture into three bowls. Add a different food coloring to each bowl. Stir.

6. Place a tiny bit of frosting on a cookie. Drag a toothpick out from the center of the frosting. Make it look like a firework. Add another color of frosting the same way.

7. Repeat step 6 to decorate the rest of the cookies.

spooky
eye
candy

INGREDIENTS

3 eggs
¾ cup white sugar
red and yellow food coloring
½ cup powdered sugar
½ cup semi-sweet chocolate chips

. . . .

TOOLS

baking sheets
parchment paper
mixing bowls
electric mixer
pot holders
measuring cups
measuring spoons
spoon
pot holders
mixing spoon

1 Preheat the oven to 225 degrees. Cover the baking sheets with parchment paper.

2 Tap an egg gently against the edge of a bowl. Hold the egg over the bowl. Pull the shell apart. Carefully pass the egg back and forth between the halves of the shell. The egg white will fall into the bowl. The yolk will stay in the shell. Throw the yolk away. Separate the other eggs the same way.

3 Beat the egg whites on low speed for 1 minute.

4 Beat the egg whites on medium speed for 2 to 3 minutes. Stop when they become **fluffy**.

5 Add the sugar 1 tablespoon at a time. Beat in each tablespoon on high speed. Then add the next one. Continue beating until the mixture becomes very stiff.

6 Fill a spoon with batter. Put it on a baking sheet. Repeat with the rest of the batter. Bake for 1 hour and 15 minutes. Let the cookies cool.

7 Make the frosting. Put the powdered sugar and ½ tablespoon water in a small bowl. Stir.

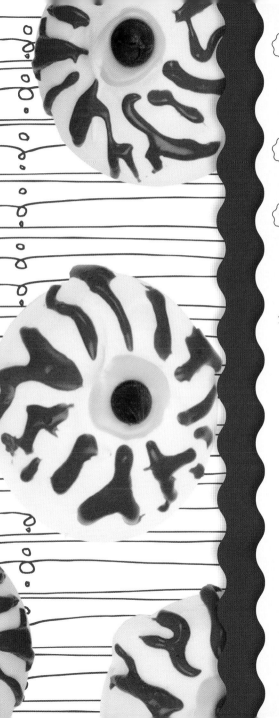

8. **Divide** the frosting into two bowls. Stir red food coloring into one bowl. Stir yellow food coloring into the second bowl.

9. **Drizzle** red icing on the cookies. Make it look like blood vessels.

10. Make a circle of yellow frosting in the middle of the cookie. Place a chocolate chip on top of the yellow icing.

11. Repeat step 10 to decorate the rest of the cookies.

sugary dreidel pops

MAKES 12 COOKIES

INGREDIENTS

blue sprinkles
1 cup white chocolate
    chips
1 tablespoon canola oil
12 Hershey's Kisses
12 marshmallows

TOOLS

baking sheets
waxed paper
small bowl
measuring cups
measuring spoons
microwave-safe bowls
12 lollipop sticks

1 Cover the baking sheets with waxed paper. Put the blue sprinkles in a small bowl.

2 Put the white chocolate chips and canola oil in a microwave-safe bowl. Microwave on high for 30 seconds. Remove the bowl and stir its contents. Repeat heating and stirring until the chips are melted.

3 Dip the bottom of each Kiss in the white chocolate. Press each Kiss onto the flat side of a marshmallow. Set them on the baking sheets.

4 Push a lollipop stick into a marshmallow opposite the Kiss. Hold the stick. Dip the marshmallow in the white chocolate. Coat the marshmallow and Kiss.

5 Cover the marshmallow with sprinkles. Put the marshmallow on a baking sheet.

6 Repeat steps 4 and 5 with the rest of the marshmallows. Put the baking sheets in the refrigerator for 15 minutes.

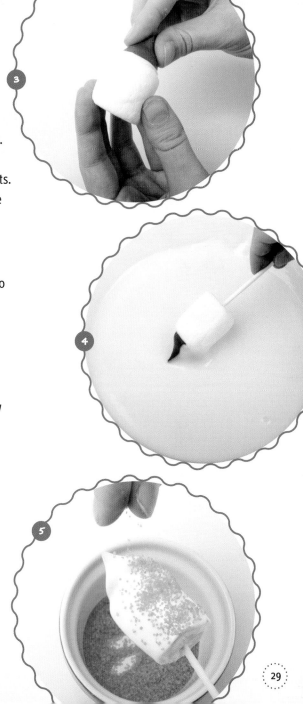

29

candy
cane
twists

MAKES 12 COOKIES

INGREDIENTS

2½ cups all-purpose flour

1 teaspoon salt

½ cup butter

½ cup shortening

1 cup white sugar

1 egg

1 teaspoon peppermint extract

1 teaspoon vanilla extract

red food coloring

. . . .

TOOLS

baking sheets

parchment paper

measuring cups

measuring spoons

mixing bowls

mixing spoon

electric mixer

cutting board

pot holders

spatula

cooling rack

1   Preheat the oven to 350 degrees. Cover the baking sheets with parchment paper.

2   Stir the flour and salt together in a medium bowl. Put the butter, shortening, sugar, egg, peppermint, and vanilla in a large bowl. Mix with an electric mixer. Add the flour mixture to the butter mixture. Mix well.

3   **Divide** the dough into two bowls. Mix red food coloring into one half of the dough.

4   Place 1 teaspoon of dough on a cutting board. Roll it into a 4-inch (10 cm) strip. Add flour to the surface if the dough sticks. Repeat until all of the dough is rolled into strips.

5   Twist a red strip and a white strip together. Place it on a baking sheet. Repeat until all of the strips are twisted into candy canes.

6   Bake for 9 minutes. Put the cookies on a cooling rack.

TIP

If the dough is **crumbly,** add 1 to 2 tablespoons canola oil. Mix it in with your hands.

GLOSSARY

amazing – wonderful or surprising.

container – something that other things can be put into.

counter – a level surface where food is made.

crumbly – easily broken into small pieces.

delicious – very pleasing to taste or smell.

divide – to separate into equal groups or parts.

drizzle – to pour in a thin stream.

fluffy – light, soft, and airy.

layer – one thickness of something that may be over or under another thickness.

permission – when a person in charge says it is okay to do something.

recipe – instructions for making something.

slice – a thin piece cut from something.

towel – a cloth or paper used for cleaning or drying.

utensil – a tool used to prepare or eat food.